SIFTING THROUGH THE ASHES

SIFTING
THROUGH
THE ASHES

MICHAEL NGUYEN

iUniverse, Inc.
Bloomington

Sifting Through the Ashes

iUniverse books may be ordered through booksellers or by contacting:

iUniverse
1663 Liberty Drive
Bloomington, IN 47403
www.iuniverse.com
1-800-Authors (1-800-288-4677)

ISBN: 978-1-4502-8511-7 (sc)
ISBN: 978-1-4502-8512-4 (ebk)

Printed in the United States of America

iUniverse rev. date: 01/06/2011

Contents

We Three Kings

The three of us are here for more
Of the same spinning, revolving,
Turning looking for roses delicate
Floating in semi-circles of ripples
Skipping rocks like kids of before.

We are warriors of words and phrases
Ready for battle, our armor is made
Of orange, coral, floral, metal still
Made best strong. We battle our vices
In the middle of the cavernous night.

In the middle of the outside storm
We rest next to the fire telling stories
Of where we've been and where we
Were. It's cold outside making the
Fire inside feel that much warmer.

Obscene Syndication

Blasting pin points charred under doings
Chocolate banana splits spoons sunder
Under wonder of other samplings

Chance lotto hoping wondering all night
Caramel stretch out on the T.V. Syndicated
To its full extent show slow mammal

Sex on the tube again spin turn about
Getting sick in the back no one to save
Except himself and his throat.

He finally purges himself of it all
And everyone feels better and the fool
Drives himself home defeated, tired.

Pulling Smoke

Parking spots under development structure fire
Suction back draft open doors to naivety
Roaring orange full truck plug into the corner

Smoke pulling in tempting them to drown it
No such luck simple mistake to water the center
Late night continues more of the same

After a while the fire begins to give up
The truck never gives up even through out the night
And now the call is done and the fire is out.

The people are saved despite their homes
Charred black ash grays stands delicate
With a touch of an axe it falls apart.

The embers still burn and last through,
The city calls for us to bring it down,
The crescent moon hangs low tonight.

Calling Out Sugar

Peanut butter panic in time
Of tumultuous thunder sitting
In a room running in my mind
All the way home. Honey I think
I'm in love. Again and again
We are what we are. Damnation
To all the Dunces out there waiting
To be called, "Ka Ka Ka Ka."
Call it out till they scream their turn
Chocolate covered candy for the kids
In the neighborhood, but none of them answered
A handful came but not enough to empty the bowl
Raise your coffee filled cups right up to the sky
So your sore knob knees can feel feather weights again
Drink till you pass on perfect direction
Die till you pass on a perfect will
Do nothing till you pass on an empty life

Now is Never

I am the way I hate am
Hating hot openings of other
Ways of wandering

Chocolate cocoa on a raucous rainy night
Lightning lures the thunder
Outside over the skyline

Over the outro to a story short told
To an audience left dumbstruck
Yet left in awe.

Space is near, now is never the time
And I am what I was, a man
On the town looking for more.

Splendid sipperings of a more
Natural state during this
Nocturnal wonderland

Gifts For Kids

Kindling kites in an orderly world of
A standard succulent soft bedding
Beneath other blossoming buds and
Booming babies ready to be rekindled
In a softer fashion fused together to be
Blown to bits like tiny explosions that is
Tickle me Elmos and wind up wheels
Keep up with the kids, their wants
And their necessities the moment becomes
Whatever is most needed and most of all
What is redundant.

Dry Leaves In the Air

Lost words burn to the center of it
My speech is there for you to understand
I put things away—perfect—where
I want them to be in a place where I only know
I take off my sweater waiting for
The springtime because this time I know it's coming
He licked his lips as if they were
Dry leaves in the air
He curled up into the fetal position
Just to escape.
The ambiance of the place
Makes it seem breakable,
Fragile even the seams of the blanket loosen
As he lays down
His breath leaves him as a stagnant
Motion of dead air.
He can taste the smoke on his lips
While the skin clings on for death

Staring at the Sky From the Flat of My Back

Mixture concoction flat on her back
Beer drunk black out allergic reaction
Long night sober driver
One drink is not enough
Control the private party, while one girl flirts with
Two boys even though she should choose
Left dry with luck there was no fight
The two boys knew each other deeper
As if they never knew each other
By any other night.
I make it out clean and sober
With my drunk brother next to me
Wondering if she even
Thought about me. Think twice
Double check hoping best wishes
Dream state of her beauty
Non-vanity yet left indifferent
Staring at the stars having
A smoke which distracts me enough
From the vicious grips of the
Woman.

Waifs and Other Names

Fast moving monuments claiming the
Clientele, while others consumed and
Consummated coloring kids books for
Them thus calling for a greater more
Grand look of a gust of gun slinging
A show for an audience of grandiose
Proportions picking at scabs and slicing
Ingrown nails nailing knickerbockers
To the wall wailing sports illustrated
Models growing until the next one comes
Grabbing at their clothes mixing mauling
And meandering at the shot but done
In a professional fashion un-falsely done
Fixed so quick fast enough to say it and
There she is the one.

A Day at the Park

By the early morning I sat
As the birds swoop by
As if they were hungry enough
To attack. There was a mother
And two twins.
The mother distracted me,
While the two early birds
Were set ready to attack,
I just ran away like a coward.

As I exited the park with my
News paper and coffee in hand
I stood on the curb,
While the cars roared into it
I thought back to my self
I could have fought those
Birds off with my news paper,
but oh well
They won this round
Those damn birds.

I decided not to cross the street
And instead to take the sidewalk
I noticed a couple on
A bench tingling by the sense
Of it. I thought to my lonely self
I could have a girl like that
I'd just feel awkward showing up
At a bar by myself looking for
Single woman looking for a
Single man.

Voices and Other Hauntings

It's cold
Where I am
And only where
I was standing
But now
I sit
Accepting my house
and its distractions
It is quite dark now
And I don't know
Where I am anymore.

This time I'm not scared, but I think
I'm being haunted
Even if I am brave enough
So I ask my mother to leave me with this predicament
And moving on I provoked him out
Because I am one myself

Now they don't really bother me
Anymore
Neither do the voices
I'm on the way
To recovery like
I already was.

Molding God From Nothing

All in all I think is that
I can swing the rest
Of the stay without
Any qualms or quarrels.
I should probably stay with
God in this room.

Only one person can know
About the point of view
I'm getting at during
An intense moment of action
And dense friction
And only then will I figure
Out what is there left
of the latter mass
waiting to be sung.

People cry out sick of
The boredom and time
Being spent of witling
Souls and bodies
Both one in the same
Connected in unison
Like quaint puppets or
Pompous dolls.

Ocean Of Stars

The mist flows in from the ocean
Knowing that it will dissipate
Into the air making love to each
Of its particles spinning and spiraling
Wanting control of it all.

This spin, this orbit is all that we know
Of what is left. It's cold out there
In space empty and wondrous.
I will them into existence and think
of why there are paths
By the way of falling
Towards the nebulas and black holes.

I can only think of one thing left
To say which is to let myself go
Off my rocker into the abyss
Of fluid motions and the nothing
That fills it.

A Mother's Children

I visited my family
From the east coast
And it was a good visit
They had plans for me
For which I fell right into
It turned out
To be a good trip
I even played guitar
And sang for a bit,
Which impressed them
For the most part.

We visited the Washington Monument
And the Smithsonian Museum
Which was interesting
A lot of it was based on aeronautics
They even had this flight simulator
Where you can land a plane.
I didn't think I could do it at first
But it was easier than my fear
Of being out there alone.

There was a baby,
She was about one or two years old,
She was my cousin's
She looked like a good mother
And she treated everybody just the same.

New Beginning

It's easy to forget what is
Left off especially when there
Is so much pressure to do so, which
Gives way to a new beginning fresh and un-wanting.

I thank her for the pencils she gave
Me, she says, "It writes well and it will
Give you good luck." She is
Nice because of that, and she gave
Unconditionally in the eyes of God.

And in this anti-climatic ending I can
Only force out words spilled over onto page
Catching certain phrases and thoughts.
But in this said, I could only wait
Until next time to breathe the language again.

From The Bottom of Water

Looking up from the bottom to the
Top of the water you can
See the sun glaring down in
Columns and shafts beautifying the
Breath that I released turning into
Rings.

People keep pacing back and forth
As these walls try to gain a sense
Of sane clarity or a run from the
Suffering that they left behind and
Forgot to do.

We send out messages hoping some
One will soon find out what good
We have done,
while we ask the gods
for the such.

Fishing Alone

Thin split otherwise hit miss
The kid sits up there glowing
Moving being there alone
Loving it to action

The river turns into him
He struggles for the first
Time making him a man
His first star caught…

Stars from a far close
The picture
Was there and the catch
Was his…

The Muse and Her Core

We pray
For the source
To come
Other wise known as
The core
Of all things
Seemingly invincible
We know it
As the energy of life

The stars chase
Each other
While Gods watch them
And the universal Muse will
Have her way with them
Which she didn't mind
Too much

She lacks the confidence
And that is why
She'll lose her love

Here We Go

And here we go
Ready to waste
The night away
Into the deep hours
Draining booze
We bought with a fake I.D.
But no one said anything

"I'm only in on it, when the getting's good."
And once I got something good going
People always latch on.
I used certain sayings
To pick up on girls but we failed miserably

The days of reaction grew more
And more humid making it hard to
Breath, especially near
Central Park and outside
F.A.O Schwartz Toy Co.

This Dance

There is a dance in which we
Spin tumbling down the mountain
Stretching for a branch or
Twig or something to catch our fall.

The pain starts to shoot, which in
Turn causes anguish in the
Physical sense; with this taken in
You should know more of pain itself.

The synapses firing are faster than
Before because of the adrenaline
In which, we rise out of ourselves
And in conclusion we give in instead
Of giving up.

Surroundings and Distractions

I separate from the surroundings
Distractions waiting for a more
Simple way to become an even more
Callous person resilient to anything.

This path that you sent me on
Is dangerous and precocious, while
The snakes and coyotes keep to
Themselves because there is nothing
Left for them to devour.

A blurred vision of an image used
To be in better focus than the objects
And things surrounding us including
Shrubbery hanging from trees
As the light that shines through the leaves
From above.

Across the Meadow

The dark crawls
Across the meadow
Making a shadow
Of the mountain
At night
We could celebrate
About
The fire made

It was better
Than any cabin
We could've rented
We had no
Other choice
Because father
Told us so

And in this said
Smaller beings
Around us sparked up
And showed us the ways
Of the valley
We listened to our radio
Waiting for the stars to sleep

The Noise of a Clock

Everywhere I turn there is a second
Waiting to be counted. Tick tock
Tick tock. Whether it be in class,
In traffic or at work. Tick tock
Tick tock. I love it when it's silent
Noise just living alone. But then it comes
Up again and that's all I end up doing is counting
Grueling counting other than that I feel
Strained and spent, stretched even.

Those that followed were left behind
Another step and they might fall, while
Their path is filled with time strange unique
Melting time

Faces and Staircases

Faces appear when they can't
Out of walls bursting to the seams
The surfaces are stretched from the frame
There are many of them dancing with each other

In sync they continue further and further
Into the night never resting
They always repeat the cycle they were given
Whether it be chasing each other or resting in bed

The stair cases leading up to each other
Turn in an awkward revolution to
The faces…together they move in a strange perfection of
Motion, flow, and movement.

A Collection of Light and Dark

Light and dark travel next to each other
Disappearing into a collection
Up there where she can only
Imagine creation to be.

We are stuck in this room together
With nothing but each other
And silent communication and in opening
Up this way I feel more comfortable.

We've grown distant even though
We imagine we were close. We barely
Talk to each other, other wise
Being each other is all we have.

Closest to God

I forget
The understanding
That Once
You have become
Closest To god
As you can be,
You Probably
Are and might be
The same.

And in this
Said, we know
Where We are found
And our word is
A greater force
Than that of a planet
traveling through space.

We know
Indefinitely
That we
Will exist
Beyond our time
With wrinkles
On our faces
And Stains
On our teeth.

Dependence on Face

I trim the plants until they look okay
Deeper we went into the night and day
Now we know how not to look
And I hope you bury yourself in that book
As the music comes around we talk
We come around the park and walk
We bring the birds and feathered sights
Into a world of delicate light
And here we are ready for science
We trained them enough until they soared
Sugar drinks and other refreshments are called
Into a place I forgot we saw.

We bury the ones we sow
While light hits day and we grow
Slowly as if we never did
We put on our masks to hide we hid
Burning our faces just for show
Our commitment and how we know.

This lowly cut has got me by
The heart if only we knew
How to start and we are here
For the violent attacks of oil and gears
We reap the events with things
Left soiled. Again I can't find
This place. It's probably because of
Dependence on face.

Here we are ready for more
We Leave with just an eye sore
Her lips pressed against
The window leaving a mark
To clean the slate she hunts like a shark.
She signs It neatly with out a trace, but
She's only in it for the chase.

Melting Between Speakers

I can't bear my thoughts
Anymore as if they are sound waves
From speakers blaring from
Both sides pounding my body
Into oblivion. I feel like I'm
Melting from the inside out.

There were these two kids
That kept bothering me.
I sat down to my typing class
And they sat down next to me.
They kept badgering me
And all I could do was type out
Stop can't won't now is
Not time stop broken good
Deep strain stretch apart stop
No more can't take any more
No more please stop.

All I had to do was wait
Them out just three more
Days and I'd be done
With them.
I would be tattered and finished
With, but I would be relieved
And done, nonetheless.

The Lower Dance of Grog and Music

The train blew whistles
As it glided by the blinking
Lights waiting for the
Rest to follow. The scene
Burst apart as the steam
From the engine blew past
The people waiting.

The situation ended
As the train left, while inside
The train were patrons
Figured out their positions.
The people
Who knew about trains
Got the rooms with beds,
While the other side
That still knew about
The trains went on to
To their drinks of
Brandy and cigars
Others gravitated towards
Food cabin ordering
delicate pastries and Earl Grey tea,
While once again the late
Night celebration
Continued with dancing at
The lower class cabins
Went on with drinks of grog
And fiddles and lutes.
The music was loud,
While the dance was
Louder.

The One

The music passes through
From ear to ear
With his head traveling in and out
Of skies until
He found cloud nine

He was the special one
He was expected to be
And that was why he was
He had the bravery
And confidence
Until life caught him
By the wrists

And everything started to fall apart
Now he only knows
His dark room
With no wind or land, no clouds
Just a bucket and sheets

My Brother's Gift

The moss has grown on the crown
But the diamonds show through
The stacks of CD's are a find
      And are ready to be given away to his brother

Rushing water in
      a dirty bathroom
White poodle on
      A Mother's lap
There's a kid coughing without
      An asthma inhaler
Artists struggling off of nothing but
      a S.S.I. check,
Families are getting off on bottled water
      from Costco.
African rhythms birth the blues with
      one slide note.
Orange floral reflection
      From her eye.
Green pixilation changing from
      Time to time.

When I look at a bowl of grapes, I see a bottle of wine.

I push buttons and I don't know what I'll find
A happy brother, singing to himself, being jovial as usual.
It's in his eyes you can tell
My room is right next to his
And we talk through the walls
With T.V.'s and loud stereos.

Perfectionists' Flight

There is one way I like to do things
And I've broken that routine letting
Myself fall freely into the cold unknowing
Darkness. Without light or anything other
Than the air rushing through me.

Nothing broke my fall and I never
Stopped falling. I flew through the
other side of the world spinning up
into the air. I kept hurtling and revolving
away from the planet.

Eventually I stabilized my fall and
I was stuck at the center of the Earth
With no more than my sight to guide
Me.

There She Is

I haven't talked to her
In a really long time
But I randomly saw her
In a movie
The other day.

I saw her
And she was glowing
And to be honest
I felt happy
For her
And she probably felt
The same way
About me, I hope.

We didn't
Say anything
To each other
But we acknowledged
Presence
I haven't seen
Her since
Which is
Probably better
For both of us.

Sharp Hours of Time

The round shaped bushes fed sharp hours of time
Trees filled in surroundings beneath the Earth
Today is probably more important than any other day
The taste of tea in front of me is better than before
I remember it being better.

The sun blaring as it does enough as it should
Interesting enough we are here ready for more
As we tap our feet waiting for the score
My cabin outside in the canyon of wood is…waiting.

The silence shapes my innocent ears
Which is enough to share my fears
I can't seem to lose this cough
My effort to the cause should be enough.

Obsession of Path

There are things in the way of my path
I can't seem to figure out the right route
I obsess night and day over many
Bloody spilled battles in my conscious mind
I hate that I can get away with the easiest
Blame to get myself out of a situation.

I know it's a low cowardly thing to claim
But that is just who I am a coward
With no conscious, no ego,
And I just give up on saving myself.
That's how low I've become
I am a raving Lunatic,

No one should ever meet.

I see people that belong in this world
While there is me in the corner
Waiting for someone to pick me up
Whether it be a prostitute or someone
Like one. I'm perfect for someone
To be used.

Magnolias

We see the other side of things
Waiting and waiting and waiting
For more of the same magnolia
It grows and peaks to its full
Potential coming up as if it was
Rising in a climax of beautiful fashion.
It rained that day, which cooled down
The leaves and the stems.
The buds were wet and damp.

We dig the dirt
To transfer the plant into
A bigger pot, which was
Delicate yet dangerous. We
Scooped into the pot and
Careful as it was, we did.

Now it must've been
Happier in its new home
Where the sun shone on it
And it could bud at any time
It's leaves were happy
While the roots were set to be.
We could talk to it now
We recently figure out how
We would sprinkle water on it
And it would help the plant just a bit.
We would mostly water the plant by hand
We would almost consider the plant a man.

Melting Clocks

Spins of minutes and seconds around
A clock melting on a bridge
Water rushing under
Casting alone with a pole and reel
In hand, like that kid on the moon
Fishing in space on the crescent moon.
I sit there with
A nice summer morning
All around me. I run the
Meadows free as a finch bare foot
Looking for streams to fish.
He heard about this flower
In the middle of the forest.
He alone would go on a quest
To pick it for his lover.

The forest led me through the
Darkness where there were columns
Of light shining through
He had to skip about
Rock and pebbles along the ground
And he almost twisted his ankle. He hoped
My fish wouldn't attract any
Wolves or bears, so he would have
To make it a quick trip.

It was hard, while the path
Became even much harder
To navigate. The flower is there
In sight. There is clearing

Around the grand tree with
Many growths of flowers
Around it. He pluck a few being
Sure to respect the tree and its
Growth and he packed up and
Went home.

He headed home just the same
Way as he headed there, which
Took him half the time to
Travel or so it seemed.
He gave her the flower
And she adored it. She found
The perfect vase for the flower,
Which is what woman do when
They get flowers. She couldn't
Be any happier.

It Landed in Perfection

I flicked a cigarette
At the ground to make
It dance for a second
Then it landed perfectly
In place or at least from
My point of view.

Afterwards I acquired an
Afternoon iced tea from
The local coffee joint. I
Sat their for a while
In my usual spot looking
For inspiration in the people
Around me and more
Specifically the fountain
In the middle, which
Roared on as did the wind.

I wrote down what I saw,
Which was private to me
And only me probably
Because I have a special
Relationship with them
And I want to keep their
Anonymity.

Obligation to Fear

I fear but there is
No fear inside me
Even when asked to
I can't, which is only
An obligation after a time,
And in this said we know
Little secrets about each other
To get the days by, but
As to me I kept my secrets
To myself, which make
The secrets all to their
Own.

The secrets grow stronger
Because they are kept
Deeper and deeper inside.
Churning pot of liquid thoughts
Of blue and green
The clear and white came
Through and you could
See the dreams come
About to the rim of a
Bowl.

Holy River

Holy river flows along while we're just
Nothing but a pair of aces and us
We are here for the rush of it
All I'm left with is the bit.

Money found in hand from a friend
Can't hold on to it, just too much
I probably have to end up having to send
Send it somewhere safe, which is enough.

I pinched some of it before it went.
To pay for rent, some comics, some food.
I needed more, I pinched from where it was sent
The need, the want, like staring at burning wood.

Letting One Up

There are things in the way of
Letting up another person in need
Of a dire break of supporting
Another person who is need of just
The same.

With this in mind I have to
Remind myself of my
Actions and to be careful of people
Who are invested in this much.

And without knowing you can
Further yourself more than you have ever
Known, with colleagues and peers
That have never gone as far either

A King's Decision

Dancing under every second
Of every count of the moment
Of the moon
Viscous battlement led
To unfair strenuous limits
Almost as if they were
Slaves to the war
Sent from God to prove
What other point than
Their own misled egos
They were lied to given
No other choice than
To believe in the lie
Of a councilor
There is only so much
Truth a mother can bring
To Him. It is his sense
That brings him his mad
Decisions. And the war
Roars on despite the inner
Court's bickerings.

Rush of Air From the Bottom

Opened to the bottomless pit
We stared. We couldn't do
Anything else but stand there
In catatonia. The wind rushed up
From the chasm blasting up
From the edge. We waited until
The wind stopped. It came in intervals
Like contractions from a womb of
A pregnant woman.
We propelled down even though
These gusts were blowing, they were bound to stop
After a while. The wind stopped
Just long enough for us to drop
Night sticks into the hole.
Just as quickly as the wind rushed
We quickly propelled down.
We reached the bottom perfectly.
In our eyes everything was green
We saw beady green eyes matched
With darker shades of wings.
These bodies clung onto growths
Of crystal, of which were too awkward
And too well set to retrieve.
They were here for one thing
Which was the crown diamond.
They had to navigate through
A thin corridor of walls pressing
Against them to the most unbearable
Extent, but once they got to the
Other side they found the crown covered
In moss.

Losing Oneself to Limbo

Coughing madness on a turning bed
Constant hell all night
To a day of figuring out
The problem which is worse than answering
It self.

The road bends to the yells in the back
While the speeding increases to
An illness we can't understand.
He comes home to nothing but a bed
And an oscillating fan he curls up
To a fetal position.
Thinking he can rest. His work
Waits for him, but there is no
Inspiration, no muse there for him
So he drinks himself exploring
Each room in an oblivion of limbo.

The Poison Hits Deep

Can't people be the same
Or the poison hits so deep
In the sense of effect
Spit fire hurt deep sense
Effect other than the only thing to do
Trap is to spit into the asphalt.

With the wind blasting in
The window spitting
Is quite a difficult blow
Blast other flow explode
Ignite churning revolving
Purple velvet ceiling
Melting as it is
Children yelling as
They are.

Broken Locks

I got mad the other
Day about that ponder
And I got in a fight with
A door, twisting its locks
And jamming the knobs but
I couldn't get anywhere
After wards I took a look at the
Window to the clouds and
Wondered how air clings
To the Skies and how
The clouds get locked
Some how but then again
There is a slow movement
To all that captured my senses.

The Last Time

The yells permeate through
The dry wall, as the cold air stings the ear
And the moths flutter away.
The old jacket still fits
This is the last time I will
See my friends before I jump
Out into oblivion waiting for the fall
And the landing.
I can't work with
It anymore trying to pump life into
Its lungs hoping I can recessitate
The remainders of the sound.

Out in the Desert with My Fire

I whistle to my horse and he shows
It still amazes me when he
Knows when to come.
He has white patches
On top of a brown type skin.
I hop on with a map in hand
Wandering through the brush.
I almost lose my path,
Even with this discolored,
Yellowish map.
My horse shows how tired he is
With his grunts and breathing
So I slow him down to let him
Catch up. We both stop for a while
As I survive myself through
A canteen of fresh metallic water.
There is a river
Nearby, so I decide to stop
For my horse and he drank
From her as he should have.
It's about time according
To the sun to set up camp.
The fire I create is now slowly roaring, I roast
The meat I hunted and saved,
It tastes fresh off the bone.
I doze off to bed underneath
The bowl of stars.
It was as if god
Took a pin and poked
The night sky a million
Times.

Walking Priest

Aftermath with cockroaches surviving
Nothing but another nuclear wasteland
Dust bites another one yet He survives alone
collects pieces that survives with Him
He carries the Book with Him.
He finds a town with others like Him.
He reads from the Book.
Acceptance Church Priest Choir
Hymns Verse The Book Voice
His Reading Singing

Pouring Down Liquid

There is more than enough which is there for sight
I can put sight down on liquid which is
surprising for the most part because
I'm blocked by this moss covered stone,
but I will be free.

I blast holes in the night until He answered with trickling light
it's as if he did it for me, just for me
I try and try, but I can't catch every drop
I swing my arms and spin around in celebration
it is time for me to jump; jump out of this blur
I'm free out here; free without my restraints

Tonight is a cold night probably because of the rain,
it's warmer inside while the fire roars on quietly
unnoticed. It's as if I was in a womb and she is
snowing in her hospital cabin.

The Weather Man

Thunder thoughts under which you
Never knew thinking by yourself again
Getting lost lapping up lakes of nothing
Now can be never or even be a better state
Of a striking picture of yourself

Once addicted you can't stop meeting
That mirror mastering the luxurious look
Isn't it the same way either way
It probably is and will be according
To the weather man having so much to say

This control over the masses affects us so
What is it that we trust thoroughly in an intangible sense
With pictures of twisters and hurricanes.
Distant as they are they are still a precursor of tomorrow's mood.
And that is where we halt and ask for rain.

So here's to the weather man and his anecdotes
Let there be flashy signs and even flashier suits.
The darkness is coming and the lightning will strike
Thunder will sound in the distance,
While the day will come soon enough.

Models and Chicken Bones

Funkadelic fusion from another place than here
Faster fist pumping from creeps on t.v.
Can't come near a callous coming to a perfect explosion
Counting casting calls to naked models cheating
on their boyfriends in the next room.
Complicated situations making him cry.
Sensitive as he is he does so until his eyes are dry.
Deep frying underlying eggs keep trying until you can't die.
Cheap seats between a fat man and an old lady.
I smell moth balls and greasy chicken bones.

Alone inside with scones and rye
Pastels and light, with nothing to write
Poor fellows at night, by someone who sighed.
Lost college students, who forgot to apply.

Dead commercials on the tube
Wet napkins waiting for two
Obligations never end
Broken bones will always mend.

Puke bags and other things
I can't wait to smoke and sing
Realize the touches of her hand
I hope she stays so I can be her man.

DJ's singing and bands are playing
I can't forget all the sayings
Get up going to another plane
Don't stop before I go insane.